I KNOCKED, HE ANSWERED

(LUKE 11:9 AND 10)

Pierre Poirier

ISBN 979-8-88644-670-8 (Paperback)
ISBN 979-8-88644-671-5 (Digital)

Covenant Books
11661 Hwy 707
Murrells Inlet, SC 29576
www.covenantbooks.com

I dedicate this testimony to my mother, a saint in her own right. She dedicated her life to the Catholic Church and to her family and friends.

To my sister Betty, for always being there for me and those in need.

To Rev. John McClatuh, who encouraged me to write my testimony.

To those who believe in the words of our heavenly Father; His Son, Jesus; and the Holy Spirit.

CONTENTS

PREFACE

I am giving this testimony to help and confirm the spiritual existence of the Blessed Trinity and the power of our God, Lord, and Jesus Christ, our Savior, to the skeptical and nonbelievers.

This book is based upon actual miracles given to me by the Lord. When I knocked, He answered.

My prayer to the reader is for you to know that He is there for you. Knock and He will answer.

Accept Jesus Christ as your personal Savior. Confess your sins, repent for your sins, and surrender yourself up to Him, and you too will find peace with yourself and our Lord, as I have years ago.

Faith in our Lord is necessary to achieve the utmost prize: eternity in the kingdom of heaven. Without faith in Christ, we are lost sheep wandering aimlessly throughout life.

INTRODUCTION

These miracles were given to me when I called upon the Lord for help. According to Luke 11, verses 9 and 10, Jesus said, "Whosoever knocketh on my door, it shall be opened." I've knocked for each of the miracles in this, my testimony to you. I will consent to a polygraph test or hypnosis at the requestor's expense.

I am a descendant of Jacques Poirier (born 1659 in Avon, France). He was a descendant of a French village in Israel ("Poier" during the era of King Midas). *Porier* is pear tree, and *poier* is "wandering pear" in English. Census takers in the US destroyed our real name, which is Poirier Dit DeLoge.

I was born on St. Peter's Day (September 9, 1933) and raised Catholic (christened Joseph, baptized). My communion name given was Paul, and the confirmation name I chose was Peter. I will write under the pen name Peter Porier, since *Porier* is my true surname. The Pioer was credited in AD 500, during King Midas's reign, as the founder of the Knights of the Templar. A dispute with the government ended by moving their village, Pioer, to Paris, France, where they founded the European seat of the Knights of the Templar. I was born in the village of

Malone in Franklin County, New York, the home of my family back in the 1600s.

Many of my family served in World War I, World War II, and the Civil War. My great-grandfather Bernard Barney Boyea was a prisoner at Andersonville Prison, Georgia. It was considered hell on earth. He was bayoneted in the leg then forced to sleep on the ground. He soon had gangrene in his wound, and they sawed his leg off. He had a wooden leg for the rest of his life. He is buried in Notre Dame Cemetery with the old Civil War monument. My grandfather, grandmother, and others are in their plot about thirty feet from Barney's and many others in Notre Dame.

My family on Mother's side were Boyea, Charbonneau, and Roberts. On Father's side, it was Porier, Myers, Bodreau, Plomadore, Cousins, Arquette, and so on. Many others served, even coming in from Canada to serve. My siblings (two brothers) and I were drafted. My oldest brother served in Germany. The youngest was in the army in Korea and parachuted in at Pork Chop Hill. And I was with the air force in North Korea, Japan, and many other countries. I was on the crew that flew into Sidi Slimane in 1956. The very night we landed, a civil war broke out. Arabs fought against the controlling French in Algiers. Our bus was stopped by the Arabs. We were all taken off and lined up as the man in charge read the passports. He came to mine and called me out. I stood listening for several minutes to how he hated the French as he shoved his automatic rifle into my gut.

My wing commander, a full colonel, a couple of lieutenant colonels, aircraft commanders, and other officers stood at attention, shivering in their shoes. I realized there was no help from them.

My brain screamed in my skull, "Lord, I need Your help."

The Arab said, "I want to kill you so bad. I hate you French."

I said my ancestors had lived in Canada and the US since three hundred years ago, not France.

"I hate all French," he said, poking his rifle deeper into my gut.

I looked him in the eye and said, "I don't hate Arabs, just beginning to dislike one very much. And if you want war with the US, then shoot me and start World War III."

He said, "I let you go, but I hate all French."

We took off in our DC6, and Sidi Slimane was in flames.

To this day, I have never been given any commendation for bravery. I know several officers and enlisted who should have been awarded the medal for cowardice. Our Lord, whom I called upon, gave me the strength to stand up to the enemy and survive. The war lasted for several years, and I left the air force after fourteen years of service. The realization of how my crew backed me up still haunts me today.

CHAPTER 1

My Latest Vision

2022

I was suddenly woken by a voice that said, "I didn't give you miracles to sleep on. You must finish your book so others can see what is possible. To enlighten them as to what comes after death of the body and the spiritual world thereafter."

I said I would finish it soon.

CHAPTER 2

My Mother's Passing

My mother suffered with cancer for about eight years. She was a devoted Catholic all her life. Born on November 19, 1911, she passed in 1980.

I was waking up in San Diego with pneumonia when my mother appeared at the foot of my bed. She said, "I came to tell you God has called me home. You have been a good son. Thank you for all you have done for us and others. I now know why you didn't want the priesthood but elected to serve the Lord by helping others through baptisms and helping the poor and the animals. Continue to serve the Lord in your way, and I will see you again." And she left the way she came, vanishing.

My phone rang, and I said, "I know, Betty. Mom passed."

She said, "Who called you? The hospital just called me."

I said, "She appeared to me." And I told her Mom's words.

She said, "She didn't appear to me."

I said I would catch a flight to Syracuse.

I got a flight to Hancock Field in Syracuse. We were approaching, and the captain came on the intercom, saying, "The field is closed due to a blizzard. But since we have a bereaved passenger aboard, I will make an approach. We are on final, and I don't know who this passenger is, but he knows someone up there. The runway is clear, and we're landing."

The storm was all around. It was a miracle.

After landing, he announced, "We may have to spend the night. The field just closed."

A stewardess walked by, and I got her attention and said, "Tell the captain the field will be open and runway clear when he's ready for takeoff."

I was in the terminal when a piped-in voice said, "Bill, I was never a believer. The runway is clear, and we're off to Kennedy, and you've made a believer out of me."

I heard him roar down the runway, and as he departed, they announced the runway was closed till morning and the airport was under a blizzard warning.

My niece and her husband drove us to Madrid, where my mom lay in her wake. There were fifteen minutes to spare prior to closing down. The services were well attended. It was standing room only.

I spent the next thirty days cooking and helping Dad, but not without incident. My sister Joanne and a nephew, Glenn, stayed four more days. The second day, we just finished breakfast when a loud crash came from the far end of the house. My sister went to look and called us back. The medicine chest had been ripped out of the wall and thrown out the door into the living room.

My dad said, "She told me not to move her things for a week, and last night, I emptied all of the things out of there into a bag. I guess she meant what she said."

About a week later, around midnight, I heard voices downstairs. I went down and opened the door, and Mom and Dad were sitting at the dining room table. Dad said, "Go back to bed, Billy. Your mother and I are talking."

So back to bed I went. Their conversation went on for another hour.

I spent another three weeks doing his paperwork and cooking to fill his freezer. I told him all that happened on the flight in and her visit after death. And I also told him how I prayed and asked God to clear that runway, and He did.

Dad said, "Your mother always said you were close to God and you should have been a priest. I guess she was right. In later years, she said you do plenty serving the Lord and more good than if you were a priest."

I said, "I pray for the poor and give all I can spare, sometimes going without myself, but God always takes care of me. I do His work by teaching those who want to hear the Word of God and all the blessings He's given me and baptizing those who ask."

"Your mother said you do too much for too many."

"I do nothing like what Jesus did for all of mankind," I said.

CHAPTER 3

My Father's Passing

November 1992

I received notice that my dad had passed. My roommate at the time and I—since we had three days—could drive day and night and have time to spare. We made it across without incident and arrived early afternoon. We went to the wake and spent time with Dad's attorney and so forth. The funeral went well, and we decided to leave the following day. We loaded some rockers my sister wanted dropped off in Syracuse.

I bid farewell and stopped in Syracuse, and the snow began—first blizzard of the year. I drove from Syracuse to Buffalo in heavy snow and passed by many accidents. Upon entering Pennsylvania, I noticed a restaurant on my right. I needed a rest and stopped for coffee. My arms were aching from fighting the storm and maintaining a safe ride. On the roof above the dash, we had four icons of Jesus and Mother Mary to protect us. I asked my friend Charles if he could drive in the snow. He said sure. I told him just for an hour so I could rest my arms.

The highway went downhill across an overpass and back up a hill to level highway. He started down, and I realized the road was iced over. I said to slow down. He replied, "I am only doing forty."

I told him to slow down to 5 mph. I said, "Look down in front of you. It's full of crashes. We can't get through."

A highway patrolman was waving his arms for us to stop.

Charles said, "It won't stop."

I looked up and said, "My Lord, please don't let us die so far from home and in this miserable place." Suddenly, between us was a hooded figure, no body parts showing.

Charles said, "Bill, you've changed into someone from biblical times."

I raised my arms as I assumed my guardian angel raised theirs, and we flew the van up and over the accident. I will always remember the highway patrolman and others looking up at us. We gently landed the van on the opposite hill, and my angel disappeared.

I said, "Charles, stop the van. I will drive."

He said, "I am so scared. Who are you? Are you a saint?"

I replied, "No, I am Bill."

He said, "You sounded like Bill when you spoke to whoever that was, but you're just now beginning to look like Bill. What language were you two speaking? It sounded like Hebrew."

I said, "Stop here."

And he did, asking, "Are you an angel?"

I replied, "No, just plain old Bill."

He kept saying how scared he was. I assured him he had nothing to be scared of. I said, "I called upon the Lord, and He answered."

He said, "I've never heard of someone turning into someone else as you did. But still, I knew it was you. I know who you looked like, but I can't think of his name."

I asked if it was St. Peter, and he said maybe.

I said, "Charles, do me one favor. Whomsoever will listen, tell them what you have witnessed here today. A miracle of the Lord."

He replied that he would.

I said, "I will walk around and drive. You slide over here."

I stepped out of the van and closed the door. As I went around, I noticed the snow would melt as I went by it. I got in, and Charles continued to question me as to who I really was. He added, "You're just now all Bill."

We continued on our trip, arriving safely in San Diego. He said he had discussed it with pastors, and they wanted to meet me. I declined at that time.

Until the day he passed, I would catch him staring at me. And he was never surprised as I helped those in need and baptized those I felt in my soul needed to be. He would often listen to me praying in my room and question my beliefs.

CHAPTER 4

Vernon Mager's Death

It was around 9:00 a.m. I received a phone call asking me to check on Vernon. He didn't show up for work. I went across the street and down his driveway. As I approached his driveway and his window, I could hear voices. I glanced for vehicles, and only Vernon's was there. His window was open, and as I arrived, I heard a mannish voice saying, "Vernon, we have to leave now. If we are not at the portal on time, we will have to wait for the next one to be taken up, and there's no telling how long it will be."

I said, "Vernon, the door is locked."

He said, "Bill, come in the back. Push the screen in and reach in and unlock the door."

I could hear the two other voices arguing with Vernon together about leaving for the portal. I described the voices to my friend later, and he said that they belonged to Vernon's parents.

I entered the house, and it was as quiet and cold as a morgue. Vernon was sitting on the dining room floor. He was leaning back against a chair—naked with the exception of white socks—with his head bowing forward.

I called 911, and they instructed me to put my hands around his neck and check the carotid for a pulse. I bent down and put my hands out, but I wasn't able to grasp his neck. Someone grasped my hands and put them around his neck. There was no pulse, and I notified the 911 operator. She said, "Thank you. A sheriff and a silent ambulance are on the way."

Vernon's brother heard it on his police scanner and arrived shortly after the deputy. I felt a cold rush when his brother opened the door, and I felt the spirits go by me.

A few days later, after we finished Vernon's service, Muriel asked me to come by his house for brunch. I arrived, and Muriel said, "Let's go out to the barn, and I will show you the auto I am restoring while the women prepare lunch."

While in the barn, I said, "I have to tell you my experience with Vernon and your parents the day I found Vernon." I told him what had occurred when my spirit entered the spiritual world.

He looked at me and said, "Thank you. I haven't been able to explain the tornadolike rush that came out the back door when I opened it. I was about knocked down."

I said that it was the spirits leaving to make the portal to be taken up.

He smiled and said, "Thank you so much. I feel at peace now with his passing."

I said, "Thank the Lord for allowing me to enter the spiritual world."

Vernon had just turned fifty-five a few days earlier, and I told him, "Since you're right at the max speed limit, be careful."

He said, "Strange you said that. I had a dream I wasn't going to break 55 mph."

I felt bad for days and prayed for him. We were to leave in October to tour the US in his camper. He wanted to do it so badly. Now he sees all.

CHAPTER 5

Skip and Rose Mattson

2002

My neighbors Skip and Rose lived next door to me on Sunflower Street in Bullhead City, Arizona. It was in the evening when Rose called me and asked me to come over. Skip was dying.

I went right over. The police and firemen were there, explaining that Skip, a cancer patient, had elected to die at home. They instructed us to call the police after he passed, and they would have the body removed.

Rose, Skip's sister, and I were left with Skip's dog, Joe, lying by the recliner where Skip was. I asked if Skip had been baptized. Rose asked his sister. She said no. I asked for some water. Rose brought it in, and I proceeded with the sacrament of baptism.

I asked Rose and his sister to join me behind Skip's chair. I had Rose place her hand on his head, the sister's hand on Rose's, and mine on top. They asked why, and I said, "Let's pray for him now. And when he passes, his spirit will pass through us, bidding us farewell." In a few minutes, the three of us jumped as his spirit departed for a better place.

Rose had him cremated with service at a Bullhead City Catholic church. Their three daughters, all flight attendants, arrived. Rose was skeptical about my baptism of Skip and asked the priest if Bill's baptism of Skip was good. The priest replied, "Yes, Rose, and you of little faith believe it was good."

Rose and her three daughters took his ashes to Minnesota, to his favorite fishing lake. It was early winter, and they finally found a captain with a large boat who agreed to take them out in the storm to throw his ashes.

They arrived. The captain stopped the boat, and Rose shouted, "Lord, give me a sign that Bill baptized him."

The storm calmed. The lake became placid. The captain said, "Throw the ashes."

Rose threw the ashes, and she said they formed a cross on the water. All of them went to their knees. The captain said, "Of all the ashes I've brought here, this is the first miracle I've seen."

Then the storm came back more violent than before, and they barely were able to return and dock.

Upon Rose's return home, she related the above. She asked me one question: "Why did the storm violently return?"

I looked at her and said, "The priest told you. Oh, you of little faith. Now I will tell you. You were told by the priest it was a good baptism, yet you called upon the Lord for a sign. I say, 'Thou should not tempt the Lord thy God.'"

CHAPTER 6

Semi and Auto Crash

1994
Phoenix, Arizona

We were in Phoenix to buy a truck, but to no avail.

We left Phoenix and headed home to Kingman, Arizona, during rush hour. It was bumper-to-bumper, with the exception of one car that was driving very aggressively, cutting in and out and forcing its way through the traffic.

Suddenly, I saw an 18-wheeler riding the center divider concrete enforcement. Pipes came at us like arrows, striking our windshield. The 18-wheeler had crossed lanes, and a Maricopa County truck was pinned between his cab and trailer.

The 18-wheeler came down and landed on the aggressive vehicle in front of us. A huge portable generator broke loose from the pickup and came flying straight at us. Once again, I called upon the Lord to save me. The van sped up, and the generator struck right above the windshield, ripping a hole into the roof. We went under the cab of the truck, diesel fuel running down upon us. We then hit the car ahead of us that the truck had landed on, spinning it around, and we stopped in the far lane. The next thing I remember, I was at the squashed car giving first aid to the driver, but he was deceased.

I felt someone tapping on my shoulder. I turned to see a woman. She said, "Sir, you had better go and sit. You're quite white. I am a doctor and will take over now."

After six hours, we were released to go. Our vehicle was taken, and some repairs were done to get us home. I thanked the Lord for answering my knock on His door once again.

CHAPTER 7

My Dog Cubby and Me
My Miracles

Railroad travel over the Grass River.

It was in 1946. I was told by my mother to never walk over the river on the railroad trestle. It was an afternoon when I took my German shepherd for a walk. While walking, we came to the forbidden trestle. I decided we would cross and visit Billy Wilson on the other side. We were halfway across when the unwelcome train, blowing its whistle, rapidly approached us. We were over a pier. I made Cubby lie on the ends of the ties. I grasped my hands around the end of the tie and hung over the river. I asked the Lord to help me.

The train was a long one. As car after car rumbled by, my arms were giving out, and it was around sixty feet to the rushing river below. I asked God to give me the strength to hang on. At thirteen, I was too young to die.

The train passed. I had no strength to pull myself up. I asked our Lord for help and found myself lying on the trestle. My dog Cubby was barking and pulling on me. I stood up and noticed Cubby's tail lying on the trestle. I picked up the tail and went home.

I sat on the back porch. My mother came out and asked what happened to Cubby's tail. I replied that it fell off. After some thought, she said, "You went across the trestle, didn't you?" I confessed and never crossed it again.

My dad took it and hung it on the antenna of the '34 Chevrolet. Cubby looked up at it and whimpered his satisfaction. I had sore buttocks for a few days, and I thanked God for lifting me back up to the tracks.

CHAPTER 8

Charles Cole's Passing

I made a promise at the time Charles's father passed that I would care for him. He was my best friend and companion.

I took him to his doctor's appointments and so on. He was diagnosed with cancer in approximately 2008. I took him to chemotherapy every day for at least two years. His doctor made arrangements for a stem cell transplant at Barnes Jewish Hospital in St. Louis, Missouri. I drove him there a few times until the decision was made that he was a candidate for stem cells. He spent one month there during the procedure, and since I was his caretaker, I had to spend five weeks there. Living in Missouri was just too much for me. The snow and wheelchair just became pure exhaustion. I had to load him into the back of a van, go through from the front and put him into the bed, cover him up, and secure the wheelchair when we arrived. It was unloading him and reloading him to go home.

We checked for a warmer place and read online that Pahrump, Nevada, had a cancer house.

I flew out, bought a house, flew back, and moved here. We went to the so-called cancer hospital, only to find it had been closed for a few years, yet it was still listed by Pahrump Chamber of Commerce. I began driving him to Comprehensive Cancer four times a week. The stem cells didn't work.

I drove 150 miles four times a week for a year and a half and went through two surgeries with him. He was eventually placed at Kindred Hospital. I drove back and forth 275 miles daily for over a month.

The treating physician asked me to sign off his life support. I was in his room, praying to the angel of mercy for guidance. I looked up, and a giant angel was at the head of his bed. I asked if I should do the doctor's wishes. All around the backside of his bed were smaller angels.

I knew then it was time for him to go home to Jesus.

I drove home and got the call of his passing. I fulfilled his wishes and had him cremated and took his ashes home, where I held a memorial for our friends.

The third night home, at 1:10 a.m., his CD of Mozart came on. I went into his room, where his ashes were, and told him to stop. I shut off the CD and went back to bed, and within three minutes, it was Mozart once again. I went back to his room, and

I said the next time, Mozart would be broken and would go straight into the garbage. It stopped. Every night for a month, I prayed for the forgiveness of his sins. Only twice more did he play Mozart.

I was praying for him and noticed the hallway from his room to mine was all aglow. He came toward my room, glowing, carrying his favorite hat (a white Greek fishing hat). He came into my room, stopped in front of a mirror by the door, and put the hat on. Then he turned toward me, smiled, and waved good-bye. And he was gone.

I spent the next hour praying and thanking the Lord for taking him home.

CHAPTER 9

My Fourteen Years in the US Air Force

I joined the US Air Force in 1951 in lieu of getting drafted. I went through tech school in Biloxi, Mississippi, and from there to Great Falls, Montana. After multi-engine schooling, I was assigned to a flight crew.

I recall the day the pilot didn't read the NOTAMs (notice to airman). We were flying over Fort Lewis, Washington. I heard a *boom*! I said, "God help us." The firing range was on a NOTAM as hot. The flak hit under the wing where I was sitting, shredding the underside. If it had been a fraction of an inch higher, we would have lost the wing and crashed. I thanked God for saving us and for our safe landing.

I soon found myself assigned to Tokyo, Japan. I did fly over Korea and became a Korean War vet. We were on our return to Tokyo between Wake Island

and Tokyo, over the Pacific. I was in my seat when we plummeted straight down, losing ten thousand feet or more. I said, "God, please help us." We were close to the water when we went straight back up to our cruising altitude. I lost both eardrums, but they healed back. Thanks to God for saving us all on that day.

1956
Sidi Slimane, Algiers, and Buenos Aires, Argentina

I was assigned to McQuire AFB, New Jersey. I was assigned a flight to Rhine AFB, Germany, with an overnight rest at Sidi Slimane, Algiers. We landed in Algiers and went by bus to our hotel. That evening, the Arabs started a revolution against France, who controlled the Algiers. We were notified to leave immediately. We were loaded onto a bus and were on our way to the airport. We soon encountered a roadblock by the Arabs. We were taken out of the bus and lined up alongside the bus. The Arab soldier in charge started at the end of the line where two French nationals were held at gunpoint. They were soon told "I hate the French" as they were executed. He soon made his way down the line and arrived at my flight crew. He went through our passports and said, "Who is DeLouge?"

I said that was me, and he said, "I hate you Frenchmen."

I thought to myself, *Oh, Lord. Help me now*. I replied with my name, rank, and serial number.

He replied, "I hate all French."

I replied, "I don't hate all Arabs, but right now, I am beginning to dislike one."

He said, "I hate all French and want to kill you."

By this time, the rifle was pressed tighter into my stomach. I said, "If you shoot me, you may have US forces wiping you out by morning." Then I visualized Jesus above him with His arms open. I said, "Thank You, Jesus."

And the rifle was out of my stomach, and the soldier said, "I let you go, but I hate you French."

I noticed our wing commander, a colonel, two majors, and a captain never said one word to defend me. We continued out of the airport and lost no time in taking off. The city of Sidi Slimane was engulfed in flames as we climbed on out, and I said, "Thank You, my Lord, for protecting me."

I had similar incidents when I was assigned to Buenos Aires, Argentina. I was in the Hotel Continental when hundreds of Argentinians swarmed the streets, throwing rocks and breaking windows. I said, "Lord, what should I do?" Then I realized I had written on a bedsheet "Yanks Go Home," and I hung it out of my window. I was spared as rocks and firebombs were thrown at the hotel amid chants of "Yankees, go home."

Soldiers finally forced them away. Thanks be to God. I guess they didn't appreciate us or our US aircraft flying out of their airport.

CHAPTER 10

Baptisms

I've always believed in God, the Lord, and Jesus Christ, the Second Trinity—the first being the Father, the Son, and the Holy Spirit.

If we have faith and belief in the spiritual life and have hearts full of love, then there will never be room for hate and evil.

I've always asked the Lord to help me serve Him, and through my baptisms, I've saved many souls for my Lord. I might add that when I baptize, I always ask the Lord to allow John the Baptist to assist me in the sacrament of baptism. I was asked once if John was there. I answered that I felt his presence, and Father John just smiled.

After these and many other times throughout my life, the Lord has answered when I've knocked. I know there is a beautiful heaven awaiting us who believe. Many may have opinions. However, I will continue to serve Jesus by helping the poor and needy, for all I am and have come from Jesus.

C H A P T E R 1 1

My Grandson

While I was stationed in Tokyo, Japan, I met a young Japanese woman about my age, early twenties. We were soon living together.

I was called into the commander's office, and he said, "I have a letter from your girlfriend in Helena, Montana, and she says she is pregnant with your child. What are you going to do about it?"

I said, "Go back and marry her."

He said, "I knew you would be a man about it. I will give you ten days, and you will be authorized military flights."

I said, "Thank you, sir."

I caught a military aircraft into California and had to buy a ticket on Frontier Airlines to Montana. We got married, and I returned to Tokyo, Japan. I went to my girlfriend's house. She was so excited and said, "I'm pregnant." I told her what had happened. She was quite upset. I was transferred back to the

US. I told her I would send money each month. She wrote all her information down.

I met my wife in Montana. I asked where the baby was. Her sister said she was never pregnant. She only wanted the allotment check. My wife said, "I wanted you."

We went to Trenton, New Jersey. I went on a flight to Germany for several days. On my return, I looked for my envelope from Tokyo. I asked if she had seen it. She said, "I put it in the metal bucket by the garbage. I went out and looked in the bucket, and it was all ashes. I lost all my information for Japan.

From 1954 to 2018, I heard nothing. In the interim, I was divorced in 1956. But in 2018, a so-called friend ripped me off for a car and about $5,000 in tools. The sheriff found them and told me to call them, and I was to meet them there with a tow truck. I decided to go out first. All my tools were sold after the deputies left. The neighbor told me the thieves held a big tool sale, and they left after the sale.

I notified the deputies.

I went back to have another look in a couple of days. A nurse and her Japanese boyfriend had moved in. It turned out his mother was from Japan. She was one of ten siblings. After talking to him, I realized he could be my grandson. I decided I would help them out, which I did for a year or so. They were in luck. Dan found a way to continue his job in Las Vegas, commuting daily. I sold the last of my houses in Pahrump. Dan wanted me to stay with them in a spare bedroom. I did, which helped them with rent and the like.

I decided I would ask the Father if Dan was my grandson. I went to sleep, and in a couple of hours, a voice awoke me and said, "You asked if Daniel was your grandson. I say to you, if he is, he is. If he isn't, he isn't. I say to you, treat him as he is."

I said, "Thank You, Father. I will." I told Daniel what the Father said, and he calls me Grandpa once in a while. He and Ya Yo have treated me well.

Both are working. Now she's an RN, and he works in a lab making medicine.

His mother, Auntie Ya Ho, and her two girls and I bought a trailer, and we all live together. I took the Father's words, and if Dan is or isn't, I love him as he is.

If you have problems, knock, and He will answer. You will find peace within yourself. And you must have faith, for without love, peace, and faith, you're just another lost sheep wandering aimlessly through life. Remember, we must obey our heavenly Father's laws, the Ten Commandments. Have faith in the Blessed Trinity (Father, Son, and Holy Spirit), and you will gain eternity in the kingdom of heaven and be a sheep within His flock.

CHAPTER 12

My Bible

I study my 120-year-old Bible whenever I can. Since I'm eighty-eight, it's kind of worn and tattered, but the words within are the words of God, unchanged.

I always shed tears when I open it up, knowing what He went through so we would be taken up to be with Him.

I think of what He went through for me and you. Would any of us, my brothers and sisters, go through what He went through—give our lives to save me and you?

Now I know why I cry when I read His words. They were said for the love He had for the living and the dead.

Let us find peace within ourselves, and we will have peace with Him, and our spirits will rise up to Him again.

CHAPTER 13

My Teacher

All souls in all mankind came from the heavenly Father. Therefore, regardless of race, color, or creed, every man I meet is my brother.

Every woman I meet is my sister.

Every child I meet is my child.

We are all family, and all our lives and spirits matter.

Our bodies are temples housing the Holy Spirit, which we must keep free from sin and return to the Father as it was received by us.

My teacher—the greatest teacher to walk the earth—is Jesus Christ.

CHAPTER 14

The Son Shines on Us

March 20, 2022

I know the Son shines down on me. I feel His love and compassion shining down on and inside of me.

I ask Him for forgiveness when I know He is near and to please cleanse my sins from my soul.

May all mankind accept Him as their Savior, confess their sins, repent, and place their faith and love into Him.

Think of all He did to free us all of original sin so we can see Him when we rise up to Him.

The Son shines down on you and me. Read the Testaments and believe in Him, and you will hear and see Him again.

We must surrender ourselves to Him and free our souls of sin. And when our time is up, He will take us up to see Him.

If we all have hearts full of faith and love for Him, there will be no room for hatred and sin.

Time is drawing near. Don't wait too long, for the fulfillment of His testament draws near.

Remember what He said, "I will come quickly, for I am Alpha and Omega, the beginning and the end."

Thank You, Jesus.

CHAPTER 15

Suggested Reading

Concerning His Son, Jesus Christ our Lord, which was made of the seed of David, according to the flesh. (Romans 1:3)

I say unto you, ask and it shall be given you; seek and you shall find; knock and it shall be opened unto you.

For everyone that asketh receiveth; and he that seeketh findeth; and to him that knock-eth, it shall be opened. (Luke 11:9–10)

For the woman which hath a husband is bound by law to her husband so long as he liveth;

but if her husband be dead, she is loosed from the law of her husband.

So then if her husband liveth, she be married to another man, she shall be called an adulteress. (Romans 7:2–3)

For any man that heareth the words of this prophecy of this book addeth to or taketh away, God shall do unto him as is written in verses 18 and 10. Read and heed. (Revelation 22:18)

Let your women keep silence in the churches; for it is not permitted unto them to speak; but they are commanded to be under obedience, as also saith the law.

And if they learn anything, let them as their husbands at home; for it is a shame for women to speak in the church. (1 Corinthians 14:34–35)

Read also John 5 and Revelation 22:11–21.

CONCLUSION

My life hasn't been a completely religious one. Prior to my mother's passing in 1969, I considered God's work as helping the poor, the weak, the cold, the hungry, the sick, the dying, and those incarcerated wrongfully. When she transformed at the foot of my bed and spoke to me, my religious outlook was changed from then on.

All my life, I always tried to do good. I assumed I was going down the road of life, and the end would be at the foot of the empty cross, and Jesus would be above it with His arms open, welcoming me home. Contrary to this, during my life on that road, I took detours I shouldn't have, but God always put me back on the heavenly road. I've tried to stay on it since 1969. I can only pray that I will not take any more detours, however tempting and attractive they may be, and that Jesus will give me the strength to resist temptations. Even recently, I've come face-to-face with it, but Jesus gave me the logic and strength to overcome stooping to their level. I continue now to be above those who need our prayers, and instead of lowering themselves into the pits of evil, they too will rise above anger and sin.

We all pray for most of our lives. My prayers have always been the Lord's Prayer followed by the Act of Contrition, adding, "I forgive all who have trespassed against me and pray for the forgiveness of those I've trespassed against." I then pray as follows:

> Bless the weak. Let them be strong with faith in the Blessed Trinity.
>
> Bless the hungry. May they be nourished with love for Jesus and filled with the Holy Spirit.
>
> Bless the cold. May they be warmed by the Holy Spirit and their love for Jesus.
>
> Bless the poor. May they be rich with the knowledge of Jesus and overcome.
>
> Bless those with addictions. May they resist through prayer with Jesus, faith, and love.
>
> Bless the sick and the dying through their prayers and faith in Jesus. May they be healed and live to serve God.
>
> Bless those who have been incarcerated wrongfully. May they be exonerated and set free.
>
> Father, I ask in the name of Jesus, my Savior, that all mankind will accept Jesus as their personal

Savior, confess their sins, repent for their sins, and surrender themselves up unto You. They will find peace with themselves and with Jesus. For when our hearts are full of love, there is no room for hate.

My visions have been many—some so beautiful and beyond imagination and as real as life itself. Then those with my own shortcomings. If I should detour off the highway to the foot of the cross, where Jesus will call us home with open arms, welcoming us into the spiritual heaven our Father promised all of us.

May all who read this be blessed throughout the remainder of their lives on this earth by the Father, the Son, and the Holy Spirit. My prayers are for all mankind—the living and those who have passed on. Life is so short. Eternity is forever.

My poem called "Mother's Day" was published, and I am in the International Library of Poets and the Pan-American Library of Poets.

ABOUT THE AUTHOR

Pierre Poirier was born on a farm outside of Malone, New York. He is a direct descendant of Jacques Poirier of Avon, France, in the 1600s. He was born on September 9, 1933, on St. Peter's Day, at 6:10 p.m. He spent fourteen years in the US Air Force on a flight crew. He has degrees in advanced communications, electronics, and personnel management and administration. He is a commercial flight instructor (aircraft land and sea, instrument rated). He was baptized in the Roman Catholic Church, with First Communion and confirmation. The author chose St. Peter's for his confirmation.

9 7 9 8 8 8 6 4 4 6 7 0 8